MARTHA'S
VINEYARD

MARTHA'S VINEYARD

Photographs by Alfred Eisenstaedt · Text by Henry Beetle Hough

A STUDIO BOOK · THE VIKING PRESS · NEW YORK

First published in 1970 by The Viking Press, Inc.
625 Madison Avenue, New York, N.Y. 10022

Published simultaneously in Canada by
The Macmillan Company of Canada Limited

SBN 670-45896-1

Library of Congress catalog card number: 71-100971

Printed in Belgium

To the memory of
Elizabeth Bowie Hough and De Wolfe C. Thompson

MARTHA'S VINEYARD

Three white frosts on three successive mornings were taken by old-time Vineyarders as a sort of scriptural ending of winter and beginning of spring. These mornings come at the end of March or in the fresh earliness of April, and they are recognized by more than the rime glistening on the doorstep and the branches of the lilac bush.

Characteristically, the air is still, the sun well up by six o'clock. The sun's warmth, quickly gaining, becomes mingled with the chill of the clear night past and the cold breath of the waters around the island, producing once again a long-remembered experience of renewal. Vineyard Sound lies in streaked idleness, in an elongated pattern of lighter and darker shades of blue expressing the will of the tides, the early light, and the gentleness of a new spring.

The dawn chorus of robins comes a week or two later, though some experimental chattering may have been heard earlier. Most of the friendly din of the morning is voiced by the first returning migrants, the redwings, with their incessant kree-kree-kree from the treetops and swampy borders, and the cardinals, whistling and putting into indescribable song the quickened vitality of the season and of their own flashing color.

Once there would have been the smell of freshly turned earth—some old-time Vineyarders planted their potatoes in March—but most farming has fallen before the competition of the mainland. It has been almost half a century since Mayhew G. Norton ground his corn and buckwheat and rye into meal in a windmill atop a shed identified by the quarterboard of the wrecked vessel *Elisha Gibbs.* He was probably the last. Used farmlands have surrendered slowly to thickets of bayberry, huckleberry, and sumac, and to the spires of young cedars, showing, in April, a fair prospect of reddening and budding twigs.

A visiting Kentuckian and distinguished Harvard geologist, Nathaniel Southgate Shaler, was so delighted with this colorful effect when he bought a tract on the North Shore in 1888 that he wrote: "There are many landscapes in the unhistoric wilderness endowed with a far greater share of pure natural beauty than that of the Val d'Arno or the Plain of Marathon." And in one of his notebooks: "No other landscape known to me has so many contrasted slopes in an equal amount of profile; the result is an impression of dignity totally disproportioned to the actual altitudes. . . ." He sought a civil wilderness, and found it in the island's abandoned farms with their decaying solitary houses.

Not all the old houses were gone then, leaving only their stone doorsteps, cellar holes, and lilac bushes to mark the centuries of sheep raising and husbandry ashore and the era of oars and sail in Vineyard Sound. But some were still the homes of old families, and some the beloved reward of city dwellers who had wanted, like Shaler, to possess some part of the earth and upon it a dwelling—not for one season, but for always.

In other Aprils, abroad among the hills and in the countryside of rail fences and overgrown stone walls, the cherished scent of wood smoke might have come from the hearth of a Vincent, Luce, Mayhew, Norton, Manter, Cottle, or Flanders—all old Vineyard names—or from the newly kindled fire of adopted islanders arrived early for a restorative weekend.

The white frosts of April are soon reduced to a sparkle, as the sunlight falls differently on church steeples and rooftops of the towns, flushing at first with pink-gold, then assuming utmost clarity, yet without a trace of glare. In the streets, one encounters those who are strangers, yet not strangers really, for they too, like the redwings, are familiar migrants.

Some come to inspect summer houses closed through a long winter and waiting now to be aired, to be swept of the husks of dead wasps, and to have the rooms brought gently alive for months of vacation ahead; and some come, though fewer each year, to taste the fresh-caught herring and its red roe from Mattakeesett or Chappaquansett or Gay Head. The taste for herring in spring, deeply implanted among past generations of islanders, created the same sort of recurrent longing that led exiles, later in the year, to write orders for the Vineyard's own white turnips.

An island prospect.

Herring, and whales, run far back in island annals; their part in the history of the inhabitants has been long and influential. A tradition, discredited by historians, relates that John Pease and a handful of settlers came to Edgartown some years before 1642, and the first act of the Indians was to show John Pease their herring weir. Thus the fishery figures in island life even before its recorded history, which begins with the arrival of Thomas Mayhew, Jr., in 1642, presumably in spring, when the herring were running and the wild pear was about to bring the first white bloom to the woods.

The name of Mayhew was not officially linked with herring in the records until 1665, when young Mayhew's father, the Governor, sued Joseph Codman in the court of Great Harbour (as Edgartown was first known) for "taking fish at Mattakeese" without proper authority.

Arriving in early April by air, the traveler looks down upon a winter-bare island representing the almost unadorned workmanship of the final glacial age. Spring possesses the air, but there is little green on the earth except in upisland valleys and in the pines of the State Forest, an oasis in the broad plain of frost-blackened scrub oak. They say this low plain, from which the blue hills of Chilmark may be imagined as a mountain range, was forested once with conifers. Were they cut down or were they burned?

Fires on the plain were once common, some resulting from the carelessness of outlying farmers and householders who burned their leaves in spring, and others from the ambitions of those who wanted an excellent huckleberry and blueberry crop. The roots of the scrub oak withstand fire as those of no other tree, so its patient growth has settled the character of the plain for many generations—and contributed to its extreme tardiness in the spring.

To the overhead observer, the triangular shape of the island is clearly apparent; two lobes of the glacier formed a mold, one front pressing its force and burden on a line from West Chop to Gay Head, one front approaching on a line from Tashmoo to Chappaquiddick. On these lines the advance of the ice halted and, melting, left the boulder-strewn North Shore hills, the varied landscape that Shaler loved and wrote about, and the lesser deposits facing toward Cape Cod and the sea beyond.

Waters flowing from the melting glacial ice formed the outwash plain and great ponds with long finger-like coves which are separated from the Atlantic by barrier beaches that, upon occasion, have been broken through by storms or opened by islanders to regulate the depth of the ponds and to promote the fisheries or the crops of marsh hay.

In winter there were eels to be speared or trapped by the early settlers; at other seasons when conditions were right there were perch and bass to be seined, and in a long succession of springs the vitally important herring of Pocha, Menada, Tashmoo, Gay Head, and Mattakeesett helped to shape a way of life. A map of 1783 in *Letters from an American Farmer* by Hector St. John de Crèvecœur shows "the great beach against which the Sea continually beats" and, from the westerly recess of Katama Bay to the easternmost ponds, a "herring brook."

This was the first Mattakeesett Creek, dug in 1728 and 1729 from the bay to the fresh waters of the Great Pond to form a safe channel for vast numbers of alewives returning to spawn. That first creek also made use of two minor ponds, Monoquoy and Cracktuxet, which were extinguished in the nineteenth century by the erosion of the unremitting winds and surf. Shaler thought that at one time all the ponds along the South Shore were probably connected, forming an inland sound nearly the whole length of the island.

The action of the sea, implacable though it may be, is not consistent; between the advances of great storms there are lulls during which dunes form and a balance seems almost secure. The attack of the surf, motivated by prevailing southwest winds, falls at an angle rather than frontally, so that it carries great quantities of sand from west to east. Channels cut from the ocean into the ponds or into Katama Bay therefore tend to travel eastward as the sand fills in on one side and the tidal flow cuts away on the opposite side, until at last a cycle is completed and the opening closed.

The first Mattakeesett Creek was well back from the ocean. Scenes at the creek in early spring were lively; the glint of lanterns showed through the chinks in the creek house as men and boys waited for the herring to run. As the cry, "They're showering!" came from far down the mile-long creek, all hands rushed to the scene.

Above and overleaf: South Beach.

In later years, the fish were driven up the creek with sticks, so that the oncoming alewives drove ahead of them a wave nearly a foot high. The creek house was provided with bunks, but it was hardly safe to fall asleep: the slumberer was likely to be awakened by being hauled bodily up to the rafters with a rope around his ankles. Or someone might stuff up the chimney with hay, creating a smother of smoke, and thus cause the startled sleeper to awake, choking, and dash out of doors, only to fall into a skillfully placed pail of water and slime.

Between 1836 and 1847, according to available records, the average annual herring catch was 1270 barrels, or probably not far from 700,000

herring a year. This meant a yield of $5000 or even more—at a time when schoolteachers were paid $12 a month, a house could be rented for $100 a year, and three tons of coal cost $5.

But the South Beach continued to move; its sands marched eastward to join the offshore shoals and the wasting at Wasque Point, the seaward end of Chappaquiddick. At length, the overshot of surf put the herring creek in peril. Adverse human forces were at work, too, for the Mattakeesett fishery constituted a monopoly, limiting the use of a tremendous natural resource for the profit of a special group.

In December 1855 the pond broke open to the sea, and until the beach closed again the creek was rendered useless. Restored to productivity in 1857, it yielded 1038 barrels and revenue of $4232.

In late November 1862 insurgents living on the plain opened the pond to the sea so that the floodwaters flowed directly into the ocean. For two years seining, eel-spearing, and fishing with hook and line were not limited by lease or franchise. Again the beach closed, and the herring fishery, after a fashion, was restored, but on a moonless night in 1868 the lawless digging was repeated.

Benjamin F. Butler, appearing as counsel for the beach-diggers, won acquittal on the grounds that the creek was so nearly obstructed with sand that there could be no free flow of water. And so, after a hundred and forty years, the old creek was abandoned, to be replaced about twenty years later by the ditch that can still be seen running in a straight but imperfect course from bay to pond. For many years this new creek exceeded the productivity of the old. But conditions changed, and the market gradually disappeared. Even the tracks made by the carts drawn across the plain to the docks of Edgartown are now almost extinguished. Not for years has the old cry sounded:

> Relieve the nets, I'm weak—
>   We've bailed a hundred barrels from
> The Mattakeesett Creek.

But many still remember that Egartown was long called Old Town, and that an Old Town turkey is a herring.

In the April afternoon, especially toward twilight and dusk, and long into the night, the chant of the pinkletinks has no beginning and no end. One of the brightest of sounds, much like the tinkling sleighbells of silver, the peeping comes from almost all moist places and is heard from afar. Pinkletinks are the spring peepers, *Hyla crucifer*; only the name is unique to Martha's Vineyard.

The name originated long ago and is as natural as the island spring itself, with its daffodils, moccasin flowers, arbutus, skunk cabbage, and all the rest. Obviously the word is onomatopoeic; it has been agreed upon, adopted, and embodied in spring currency because this is how the chant of the peepers sounds through the April air on Martha's Vineyard.

The universality of the spring sound of pinkletinks throughout the Vineyard is accounted for by the existence of a great number of swamps and marshy places, where the small tree toad is most happily at home. One visiting naturalist, Winthrop Packard, suggested that the pinkletinks were the origin of Shakespeare's Ariel, and that the booming of the heath hen, the eastern subspecies of prairie chicken which once flourished on the scrub oak plain, accounted in a sense for Caliban, the grosser spirit of the island. The heath hen lived longer on the Vineyard than anywhere else, and at last became extinct sometime between the Aprils of 1932 and 1933.

As for Ariel and Caliban, there is a likelihood that the tales of Bartholomew Gosnold's voyagers of 1602, repeated in the taverns of London, may have influenced Shakespeare in his conception and in his writing of *The Tempest*. Edward Everett Hale thought so. The production of the play followed soon after the return to England of Bartholomew Gosnold's men. Gosnold had visited Martha's Vineyard, and named it—perhaps for his daughter, perhaps for his mother-in-law, a woman of influence who had aided his fortunes.

There may have been no precedent then for christening a new land after a commoner rather than a queen or a king; but there the name stands in the margin of John Brereton's *True Relation*: "Marthaes Vineyard," with an "e" instead of an apostrophe. Use of the name "Martha" in Gosnold's family has been authenticated beyond doubt. Some historians of modern times found so many references to "Martin's Vineyard" that they were inclined to assume its correctness. But the late Emma Mayhew Whiting of West Tisbury, no mean historian herself, found that "Martin's" had been employed off-island, whereas the islanders had always used "Martha's." The contumacy of the mainlanders has troubled Vineyarders right up to the present moment.

Of *The Tempest*, Edward Everett Hale wrote: "in Southampton's house, Shakespeare must have met the drunken sailors on the one side, and the 'Gentlemen Adventurers' on the other. He heard there, possibly for the first time, of mussels from the rocks, of pig-nuts, of scamels . . . and the rest of

The ferry approaching Chappaquiddick.

the bill of fare of the Island." Further evidence of the playwright's knowledge of the island appears in Brereton's narrative: "he learned 'how lush and lusty the grass looks, how green' . . . and a trace of the unfortunate quarrel between the 'Gentlemen Adventurers' and the seamen runs all through the play. . . ."

Gosnold's stay lasted from May until mid-June 1602. John Brereton was one of the gentlemen adventurers and his *True Relation* is a basic Vineyard text, not only in providing clues to *The Tempest* but also because it includes memorable descriptions, still largely applicable after more than three hundred years: "an incredible store of vines, as well in the wooddie part of the Island, where they run upon every tree, that we could not goe for treading upon them. . . ." And: "We stood a while like men ravished at the beautie and delicacie of this sweet soile; for besides divers Lakes of fresh water (whereof we saw no end) Medowes very large and full of greene grass . . ."

Although the pinkletinks of each new April still discourse in sounds that may be taken as the fantasy of Ariel, the goblin heath hen are gone. For an account of their historic role one turns to Winthrop Packard's description, written in 1912, after he had met the spring on the Vineyard plain:

"Goblins cackled in weird laughter, whining and whimpering among the scrub oaks. Strange, hollow, whistling noises grew in the air about me, noises such as may be imitated by blowing into the neck of a four-ounce bottle. Gosnold and his crew, hearing such things, might well declare that devils were abroad. Indeed, they might well have seen them, or witches riding broomsticks before his satanic majesty himself. They came running and fluttering out of the scrub oaks, clad in brown, wearing black horns that stuck stiffly above their heads and with bags of bad dreams about their necks. Two of these bags, orange colored and round as oranges, hung about the neck of each creature, and now they danced in unholy glee before one another, now they sailed into the air on their broomsticks, and always mingled their strange actions with strange cries."

This, in the naturalist-poet's imagery, describes the spring courtship of the heath hen, a species doomed forever by a great fire which swept the Vineyard plain from West Tisbury to Edgartown in 1916 while the hens were on their nests among the scrub oak. So it was that Caliban left the Island of Prospero, of Gosnold, and of Mayhew.

Easterly from Edgartown lies Chappaquiddick, the smaller "separated island" of the Indians' name, and the Atlantic beyond. On Chappaquiddick

Above: "The separated island."
Below: Chappaquiddick Beach.

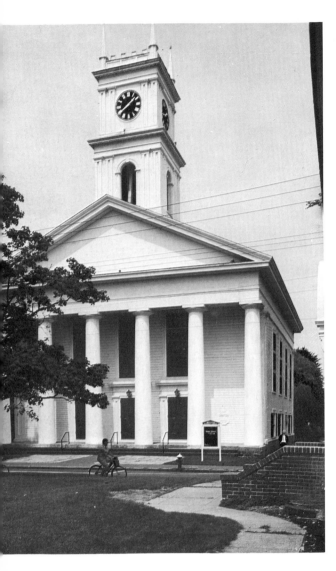
Methodist church, Edgartown.

is Sampson's Hill, ninety-four feet high, where pilots kept a lookout for approaching vessels, and where there was once a semaphore used to signal whaling news to Nantucket.

How different is Chappaquiddick from the rest of Martha's Vineyard? More different than you would suppose, though it takes a confirmed Chappaquiddicker to explain it with the required sensitivity. The distinctions are subtle and real, and have to do with shape, size, soil, the way the ground slopes and the roads reach out toward an inevitable destination of sand and surf, and even with some modifications of climate and vegetation. They also have to do with loneliness, the sense of sanctuary, independence, and tradition.

Chappaquiddick, through its ponds, barrier beaches, necks, and points, is even friendlier with the sea than the rest of the Vineyard, and for most of the year there's a real intimacy. The houses are few, yet Chappaquiddick once had its own meetinghouse, school, and hearse; it has lost these but now has its own fire station.

In spring the sunrise, showing itself far over the northern tip of Chappaquiddick's Cape Poge, reaches across Nantucket Sound to shine with particular favor on the white houses of Edgartown—and is that not one reason they were painted white in the first place, fronting shoulder by shoulder toward the harbor mouth, to reflect the gilding May dawn?

An early walker sees the daily baptism reaching such characteristic landmarks as the slender spire of the Congregational church, the clock tower of the pillared Methodist church, the Greek-revival mansion next to it, the thrifty and purposeful comeliness of the old customs house and post office, now a drugstore, at the Four Corners, and the gray-shingled magnificence—or almost that—of the John Coffin house that once looked out upon an uninterrupted view of the harbor, anchorage, dockside, and shore.

These and other buildings speak almost secretively, shyly, of the long past; only diligent inquiry brings out the stirring history of Edgartown as it was enacted by adventurous men.

Early in the eighteenth century the Coffins were sending ships to trade with the Southern states and Cuba, then to sail to the Far East for tea, spices, ginger, and the many curious things with which their great house became scented and flavored. Their story could be duplicated in the records of many Vineyard enterprises.

In the early days Vineyard voyages had lasted only a few months and were made in small vessels, usually brigs of about 150 tons, according to

Crèvecoeur. The motives that led Vineyarders to sea, he wrote, "are very different from those of other seafaring men; it is neither idleness nor profligacy that leads them to that element; it is a settled plan of life, a well founded hope of earning a livelihood; it is because their soil is bad, that they are initiated into this profession, and were they to stay at home, what would they do? The sea therefore becomes to them a kind of patrimony. . . ."

Soon, to claim this patrimony, Vineyarders were to round the Horn to hunt whales off the coasts of Chili and Japan, in the South Seas and the Sea of Okhotsk, then southward as far as New Zealand, Pitt, and Chatham, and eventually north to the Bering Sea and the Arctic, where no Nantucket vessel ever ventured.

The need for larger vessels, often of 400 tons, for the long Pacific voyages left Nantucket at a disadvantage; fully laden, such whaleships could not cross the harbor bar there, and Edgartown became a port where Nantucket whalers completed their fitting out and discharged at least some of their oil at the end of a voyage.

The first Pacific voyage out of Edgartown was made by the ship *Apollo* under Captain Jethro Daggett, which sailed July 5, 1816, to be gone twenty-two months. The ship leaked badly and there was strife on board, but she made a paying voyage. Of her crew of eighteen, including the captain's son who sailed as cabin boy, ten rose to become successful whaling masters.

Chappaquiddick alone, despite its few homesteads, was the birthplace of some forty captains during the great age of whaling. In three houses, weathered into the landscape, standing within a stone's throw of one another, lived the families of Valentine Pease, Josiah Pease, and Ephraim Ripley; of the thirty children who grew to maturity, seventeen boys became shipmasters, and seven girls the wives of shipmasters.

In 1835 the Reverend Samuel Adams Devens, a visiting clergyman, brought up to date the observations of Crèvecoeur: "out of a population in Edgartown of fifteen hundred (which number comprises all ages, male and female), about three hundred of those who have arrived at maturity—the most active and vigorous, the bone and muscle of the community, are, I may say, ever abroad and in all quarters of the globe: and further that, out of a population of three thousand on the Island, about five or six hundred cannot be said to have a home upon the land, but go down and not only go down, but live upon the sea in ships and do business, most venturesome business, in great waters."

A hundred Edgartown whaling captains appear in daguerreotypes in the

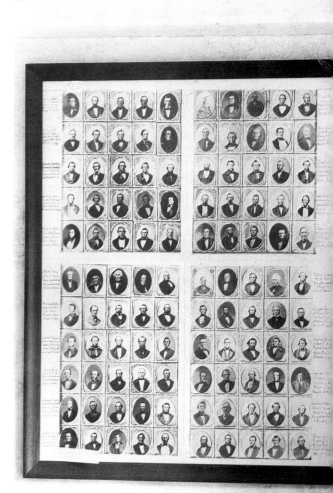

Edgartown whaling captains.

17

An Edgartown doorway.

rooms of the Dukes County Historical Society. Most of them commanded vessels from Nantucket or New Bedford or Sag Harbor, for Edgartown's own fleet was modest. The town, nevertheless, produced some notable whaling capitalists.

Timothy Coffin, whose family had long been engaged in sea trade, had amassed a fortune of $75,000 before he died in 1828 at the age of forty-two. His daughter Grace married Dr. Daniel Fisher, and they lived for a time in the gray-shingled Coffin house which still stands on Water Street, its windowpanes showing colored whorls in the sunlight.

Dr. Fisher invented a single large sperm-oil candle to take the place of the several small candles then used in lighthouses. His business soon reached a volume of $250,000 a year, and he built a mansion beside the Methodist church.

The white houses of the whaling captains on North Water and other Edgartown streets display a "harmony of roof slopes, window sashes and rhythms; a sensitive feeling for proportion and of the materials used; a restraint representing a certain elegance but good manners too," in phrases used by the architectural historian Talbot Hamlin, who also observed what others had overlooked: a candid urban character.

"There is no romantic nonsense here about country life. . . . Houses are close together and near the street; even when the houses and grounds are large, only a narrow strip, usually banked with gay flowers, separates each mansion from its neighbor and leads back to the ample tree-shaded lawns behind."

Why, of course! Edgartown planned from the first to be a city—and why not, in an age when Nantucket was third city in the state, ranking behind only Boston and Salem? These were houses of a severe but golden age, the first half of the nineteenth century. The two landmark churches were a product of the same age, the same impulse, the same oceanic tide of fortune. Strangers think of the Congregational church as having a Christopher Wren steeple, and there may be something of Wren's style in its ancestry, but the actual design was by Frederick Baylies and Jared Coffin, imposing their practicality, originality, and taste upon drawings they found in a book by Asher Benjamin.

It was appropriate that Baylies completed his plans aboard a schooner sailing Down East for lumber, because his Congregational church, built in 1828, was in essence a shipwright's church. By 1842 Baylies had turned Methodist, a denomination embraced by many of the whaling captains, and

A memento of the seafaring past in the Dukes County Historical Society museum, Edgartown.

there is a lofty grandeur in the classic pillars and spacious auditorium of the church he designed for them.

So the scenes of Edgartown, warmed by the sunlight of each new May, keep an eloquent record of the maritime age and its whaling fortunes. Only the voices have been stilled, but not entirely: one may hear in almost any spring stir of air the imagined cries of Nantucketers, noses held as if against the smell of herring, mocking Edgartown youths in the streets, gobbling at them, calling them Old Town turkeys; the voices of the whalemen at prayer meeting, gossip of wives assembled in leagues, guilds, and societies; discourses at lyceums and academies—the words of Leavitt Thaxter, seaman turned scholar, or David Davis, a governor's confidant. The ear strains to catch an almost audible creaking of old hinges, the rattle of wagon wheels, the wit and vehemence of yesterday's town meetings.

A silent record of the seafaring past is found in the burial plots, with their numerous accounts of short lives ended at sea.

Two bloody mutinies are summarized in marble. That of the ship *Globe* in 1824:

ROLAND
son of
Roland and Mary Jones
Was kill'd by the Natives
at one of the Mulgrave
Islands Feb. 21, 1824
AE 18 years
Erected by George & Mart Lawrence

Far, far from home from Friends & Kindred Dear
By savage hands this lovely youth was slain
No father's pity, or no mother's tear
Soothed the sad scene or eas'd the hour of pain

And that of the *Junior*:

Capt. Archibald Mellen Jr.
Born at Tisbury, June 5, 1830
and murdered aboard the ship Junior of New Bedford
off the coast of New Zealand, Dec. 25, 1857, by
Cyrus W. Plummer who, with other members of the
crew, had entered into a conspiracy to seize
the ship and proceed to the gold diggings of
Australia.

When Nathaniel Hawthorne rambled among the Vineyard hills one Sunday afternoon he came upon three gravestones in a secluded spot; the inscription on one still makes a lasting impression upon all who read it:

John and Lydia, that lovely pair,
  A whale killed him her body lies here;
Their souls we hope with Christ shall reign
  So our great loss is their great gain.

Of a different sort is an epitaph witnessed in the cutting by Hawthorne and described in his Twice-Told Tale, "Chippings with a Chisel":

"In strange contrast . . . was that of an infidel, whose gravestone, by his own direction, bore an avowal that the spirit within him would be extinguished like a flame, and that the nothingness whence he sprang would receive him again. Mr. Wigglesworth consulted me as to the propriety of enabling a dead man's dust to utter this dreadful creed.

" 'If I thought,' said he, 'that a single mortal would read the inscription without a shudder, my chisel should never cut a letter of it!' "

The epitaph seems gentle enough now; it speaks strongly of the stubborn individualism of those who lived by self-reliance and persisted in their own course.

It was spring when Hawthorne came to the Vineyard, and the dooryard lilacs and great lilac hedges were in bloom, the air filled with their fragrance. Like Bartholomew Gosnold before him, he was a forerunner of that latter-day island figure, the summer visitor.

By mid-May on the Vineyard the red maple tassels and the gay red filigree on the elms have given way to the tenderness of new foliage. "Plant when the maples are in full leaf," the seed catalogues have been saying through the years. Now, then, is the time. But is it really?

A cast of new color—an uncertain, delicate pink; cream, ivory, gray-green—is the first sign given by the oak woods as one sees them across old fields still tan or russet; presently they will turn, at this distance and from this place of vantage, to a yeast of foam, an intimation of tender desire, before they plunge headlong into sturdy leaf and solidity. The wild pear or shadbush shows an array of roadside blossoms; on the Vineyard the spring dance of these white petals is almost everywhere. Old-fashioned myrtle or periwinkle is awake and reminiscent in dooryards and in the places where

North Water Street, Edgartown.

21

Vineyard Haven cemetery.

dooryards used to be, linking bygone springs with this new one which hesitates uncertainly at dawn, as if dawn were a forbidden threshold.

There is truth in this fancy. The season hesitates because last night's
temperature fell into the low thirties, and on the furrowed scrub oak plain
there probably was a frost. Soon after dawn the sun has brought the mercury
up smartly, brightly, to the forties or even the low fifties, with more warmth
to come. Only early risers are aware of the consequential disagreement
between night and day that remains to be arbitrated; only they have seen the
reek of the ponds quickly disappearing.

So much is emerging, though caution remains the rule. The ferns unfold
deliberately, sassafras trees hang out their greenish-yellow blossoms as they
did for Gosnold's men. But did not Gosnold's men also put on their pea
jackets after sundown?

In Vineyard Haven the season is a week or ten days advanced beyond the
phase in Edgartown. Daffodils have bloomed earlier, the maples are dis-
tinctly ahead, one sees surer prophecies of blossom and growth everywhere.
How can one small island have different climates? The difference lies not in
any variation in latitude or longitude but in Vineyard Haven's habit of
basking on its hillside in the sun; the town nestles—industriously, but still it
nestles—beside a deeply indented harbor looking generally to the northeast,
and the land rises steeply to catch the full spring and summer sunlight in
streets and on windowpanes.

In 1835 Hawthorne was curiously impressed by the sandy streets. It
seemed to him that "the inhabitants have acquired a peculiar gait by the
constant habit of trudging ankle-deep along the sidewalks. The young girls
managed to perform it very gracefully." Perhaps Hawthorne did not know
the roll of sea legs when he saw it, or failed to allow for the steepness of the
hill.

The destiny of the town and its gait through early centuries was settled by
the convenience of the harbor opening into the great coastal highway of
Vineyard Sound. By meticulous count, some sixty thousand sail passed
through the Sound during daylight hours in any ordinary year. At Vineyard
Haven, then called Holmes Hole, the coasters took shelter, waited for tide or
wind, recruited the supplies they needed, and made good the wear of wind
and sea.

The harbor mouth lies between the two headlands that almost match,
West and East Chop. Some choose to believe they have these names because
their shapes remotely resemble two cuts of meat; almost certainly, though,

The island's quiet streets
recall Hawthorne's day.

23

Vineyard Haven, looking toward West Chop.

they were named after the jaws or chops of a vise. On each there is a lighthouse from which small craft, yachts, and ferries—but seldom now a passing schooner, tugboat, or tramp steamer—may take their bearings. The opening of the Cape Cod Canal in 1914 diverted coastal traffic, already dwindling, from Vineyard Sound.

So great was the importance of Holmes Hole to the merchants of Boston and Salem at the beginning of the nineteenth century that Jonathan Grout, a little-known pioneer in the field of rapid communication, erected a series of semaphore poles—a "telegraphe system," as he called it—on hills all the way from Vineyard Sound to Boston. Masters of arriving vessels used Grout's telegraph to report themselves to Boston shipowners, and to signal intelligence regarding cargoes and crews. But in fog or obscuring rain the system had to be suspended.

When no'theasters raged and blustered, Holmes Hole failed as a refuge, since the harbor was open to the full strength of the gales and the seas raised by them. The Lagoon, the great pond that opens into the harbor, served as a sort of inner shelter, but natural forces tended to close the connecting channel, gradually enclosing the pond behind a narrow barrier beach. In the latter part of the nineteenth century a road was built along the beach and the remaining narrow opening was bridged; but today a breakwater at the head of the outer harbor itself also provides safe anchorage for small craft.

On the east side of Vineyard Haven harbor, toward the Sound and beyond the Lagoon bridge, lies the latter-day innocence once known locally as the Barbary Coast. Eastville is its tranquil modern name, and one can hardly imagine the presence here of even the ghost of pirate, wrecker, roistering seaman, or moon-cusser. Once, though, there was a tavern here, a ship chandlery or two, a miscellany of cordage, anchors, and marine gear. Here, too, were the homes of pilots whose business included the surveying of wrecks.

It was at Eastville in 1773 that young Thomas Chase stood on the shore and watched a black, rakish ship enter the harbor and lower a boat carrying a dead man as cargo. Chase built a coffin and helped the visitors to give the body a decent burial and talked at length with the officer. The two men were to meet again during the American Revolution, after Chase shipped on a privateer as a seaman, was captured and, following an exchange of prisoners, was sent to France, where the *Bonhomme Richard* was being fitted out. There he found that his new commander was the landing officer of the Eastville burial party, John Paul Jones.

There was at least one ship chandlery on the opposite side of Holmes Hole harbor from Eastville, and the records show that on a single April day in 1889 five tugs, fifty-four schooners, one brig, five barges, and many other craft were at anchor between the Chops or near the head of the harbor.

A firm tie with the past is found in the persistence of family names on the island. When Dr. Charles E. Banks compiled a Martha's Vineyard genealogy for publication in 1925 he noted that more than a score of families who were settled there prior to 1700 were still represented by name: Allen, Butler, Cottle, Cleveland, Chase, Coffin, Daggett, Dunham, Hillman, Lambert, Look, Luce, Mayhew, Manter, Marchant, Merry, Norton, Pease, Smith, Tilton, Vincent, and West. The names preserve Vineyard flavor, not unlike the tansy and boneset that used to bloom in the dooryards, and were distributed with some exclusiveness: Pease and Vincent, Arey, Ripley, and Wimpenney belong to Edgartown; Tisbury (including West Tisbury, which was set apart in 1892) had Luce, Athearn, Look, Merry, West, and Manter; Chilmark had Tilton and Hillman and Skiff.

The names were closely linked to the island's whaling fame. There were more than 350 voyages made under Vineyard captains named Luce, Mayhew, Norton, Daggett, and Pease. And shipmasters named Fisher, a family also dating far back in island history, made more than 170 whaling voyages.

Whaling introduced other names that brought a vigorous new flavor to the Vineyard, names of men who were recruited in the Azores during long voyages. The Azoreans found here a true kinship to the islands they had left. They were precursors of a later tide which, especially around the turn of the century, established the names Amaral, Bettencourt, Silva, Maciel, Santos, and Andrade in Vineyard farms, businesses, and public office. One of the first of these was John Pray, whose house still stands above one of the steep climbs of the State Road westward from Vineyard Haven.

From the beginning, Vineyard Haven enjoyed its advantages as the island port nearest to the mainland. Before the age of steamboats, sailing packets carried passengers and freight to New Bedford and Nantucket; then came the side-wheelers with their rhythmic stride of walking beams and busy splash of paddles. A flag at the wharf "down neck" would call the steamer into Holmes Hole; another flag at the head of the harbor would denote at least three passengers and call the steamer all the way to the main landing.

In Hawthorne's day, the balance still wavered between old and new, and he wrote: "For our own part, we prefer a vessel that voyages in the good old

West Chop lighthouse.

25

East Chop lighthouse.

way, by the favor of the wind, instead of one that tears her passage through the deep in spite of wind and tide, snorting and groaning, as if tormented by the fire that rages in her entrails."

There was no intimation then of today's diesel-powered ferries breathing their own inner fire and carrying automobiles packed bumper to bumper. The new age was surely forecast, however, in the change of name from Holmes Hole to Vineyard Haven in 1871. After almost two hundred years during which it had kept a sort of longshore and nautical companionship with Woods Hole, Robinson's Hole, and Quicks Hole, an increasing sense of nicety on the part of a group of petitioners forced the rechristening of the post office and village as Vineyard Haven, although the township is still called Tisbury.

The modern age, just getting its foot in the door, leaped ahead after the great fire of August 11, 1883. The fire started in the harness factory, and as the bells rang out at nine o'clock, the townspeople—men, women, and children—tried to save what they could. It was impossible to control the spreading flames, and they swept the center of the town to the open fields beyond, leveling a great deal of the town's past in a single night.

Forty acres were burned over, and more than sixty buildings destroyed, but what burned away most completely was the past. Main Street, quickly rebuilt, reflected the eighteen eighties; the shipshape quality, the comeliness of centuries, retained now only in the streets higher on the hill, was gone from the heart of what had been Holmes Hole.

The years since have given a new quaintness to Main Street which blends with the modernity that is gradually replacing it. Those who know Vineyard Haven love the street and the town and would not have it greatly different, even though each landing ferry disgorges streams of automobiles. The traffic mocks the simplicity Hawthorne knew, but the thing that really causes anxiety is the uncertain threshold between the growing traffic and the limit of the island's capacity to absorb the vacationing crowds.

From Vineyard Haven the original State Road, water-bound, leads to the upisland towns all the way west to Gay Head. Many stone walls were ground up to make its original white macadam. Signs saying DO NOT DRIVE IN THE MIDDLE OF THE ROAD were placed at intervals along it, and shade trees were encouraged to arch overhead. In the other direction the route leads to West Chop, a place essentially Bostonian in character, with commodious summer homes overlooking the gateway to Vineyard Sound and, across the running tide, the bluff of Nobska and East Chop lighthouse.

Nashaquitsa Pond.

In the spring of 1872, with the beach plum blooming in an utter profligacy of creamy blossoms, West Chop lost its innocence of shapely dark cedars and virgin underbrush in the sophistication of a land boom. Two sea captains purchased a large tract for four hundred dollars and sold it in a few weeks for ten thousand. Hopes of further issue remained unfulfilled as the depression of 1873 moved in, and it was not until 1887 that a project to supply Vineyard Haven with water pumped from Tashmoo springs was combined with further land development.

Tashmoo, appropriately honored from earliest times, by being called a "lake" rather than a "great pond," lies conveniently to the westward of Vineyard Haven. At the head of the lake were inviting springs, providentially at hand in an age when drilling for water was not to be considered.

"Tashmoo," one of the most beautiful of the Indian place names of Martha's Vineyard, ranking with Nashaquitsa, Menemsha, Nashamois, Manaquay, and Wintucket, has been interpreted in several ways.

"The Indians did not borrow their language as we have done," wrote a scholarly island lawyer. "They made it, advancing from the concrete to the abstract by singing flights of fancy." Recalling an old deed by which the Indian Nicolas Tissimoo had conveyed land beside the lake to Richard Sarson, the lawyer-scholar penned these poetic lines:

> Now to the spring the birds of springtime come
> A'top the cat o' ninetails blackbirds sing,
> On maple branches robins build their nests,
> Beside the spring the pinkletinks trill.
>
> Now from his lodge old Nicolas comes out
> And, lifting up his voice, he sings with them,
> "We, like this spring, our hearts have overflowed.
> Lord, it is I, Kata-co-tissi-moo."

Another scholar also traced "Tashmoo" to the extended origin, "Kata-co-tissi-moo," and the meaning, "there is here a great spring of water." But a more modern historian, working with an Indian lexicon, carries the inspiration further with the translation: "In this place the heart is lifted up."

The water of Tashmoo's springs was pumped to the houses of Vineyard Haven, and Bostonians built houses at West Chop which were to be occupied for generations by their descendants. So markedly polite was the atmosphere of the colony, and so distinct did it remain amid its summer shadows, greenery, and contours, that a reputation for aloofness has grown up around it. And, indeed, West Chop came to be as self-contained as a summer place at the seashore could be, with its own beaches, tennis courts, groves, post office, cottages, casino, and a hotel, which was appropriately called The Cedars.

The community's reputation is summed up in a song written twenty years ago by William B. Dinsmore:

> Nothing ever happens in West Chop
> Which Boston thinks is the best chop.
> They saw a snake six feet long,
> They only said, "He doesn't belong!"
> Oh, nothing ever happens at West Chop.
>
> No, nothing ever happens in West Chop,
> Which Boston thinks is the best chop.
> Their only road goes just one way
> But where it goes we dare not say!
> Oh, nothing ever happens in West Chop!

Vineyard Haven harbor once extended into the deep, graceful indentation of the Lagoon, until intersected by the Beach Road and its bridge. More and more, though, the Lagoon is returning to its destiny as a safe anchorage for small craft, as well as providing a fair prospect for dwellers on Cedar Neck and on the high bluffs and slopes bordering the pond. Some find an Old World highland image in the surrounding open countryside, but the glacial kames near the head of the Lagoon, with their comb-like sandy hollows and projections, deny the kinship.

Associated with the Lagoon are place names as disparate as Webataqua, Innisfail, and Oklahoma. The pronunciation of the first, an Indian term for the region at the head of the Lagoon, is made evident in lines ascribed to Joseph Tilton, a resident of Chilmark a century and a half ago:

> Here lies Jenny, faithful slave
> Who trusted in her works to save,
> Who has paid the debt we all must pay.
> She lived and died at Webataqua.

"Innisfail," the Phoenician word for an "abode of peace and rest," was brought to the Vineyard by Tom Karl, the Irish tenor, who presided over a summer inn on the northern bluff of the Lagoon for a few summers. His guests were largely stage and concert people, with a scattering of artists; to Innisfail came Emma Cecelia Thursby and, as a child, Katharine Cornell. A forest fire destroyed the inn completely in 1906.

Why the name "Oklahoma" was applied to part of the Lagoon shore cannot be explained today, but the name is still in use.

Close behind the great spring show of beach-plum blossoms lining the Vineyard roads, crowning the cliffs, and bordering the dunes, come bridal wreath and lilac, soon followed by the crimson ramblers.

The Vineyard spring advances slowly, but summer arrives in a confident rush of sunlit days. The nights are still cool but no longer chilly, and new-comers feel refreshment in "the soft air, the broad, smooth fields, the rounded domes of foliage, together with the drowse in which all is steeped." Nathaniel Shaler, who used those words, called the Vineyard "an oasis of salubrity in our New England bad climate."

Once it was the custom for country dwellers to go to the city on the Fourth of July to witness parades, balloon ascensions, and displays of fireworks; today the whole course of holiday travel is reversed. For Martha's Vineyard the transition began when the island's whaleships were still voyaging in the Pacific.

In the warm summer of 1858, when the mutineers who had murdered Captain Archibald Mellen, Jr., aboard his ship off the coast of New Zealand the year before were being brought back to New Bedford for trial, a squadron of sailing craft from the New York Yacht Club dropped anchor at Edgartown, en route to Nahant, and remained, stormbound. For a holiday entertainment, the yachtsmen rented the town hall, paying a fee of $2.50 for the evening, decorated it with the squadron's colors and invited young women and girls of Edgartown to a gay dance. By the time the yachtsmen reached Newport on their homeward cruise, accounts of the affair were spun through with ridicule; it was even said that the piano rented for the dance was "undoubtedly the only one in town."

As a matter of fact, proud Edgartown owned a number of pianos. The first, a Chickering & Mackay, was bought by Captain Abraham Osborn in 1835, and Captain Jared Fisher had a piano in his three-story white house on North Water Street, although he cautioned his daughter from the Pacific: "I hope you will learn all parts of domestic work. The Peanio will answer sometimes it is a poor thing and should be seldom used."

The editor of the *Vineyard Gazette* denounced the departed yachtsmen—"such characters generally turn out to be better dancers, harder drinkers, and more abominable liars than any other class of men." But where yachts had come once, they would come again, particularly to so secure and beautiful

The contours of Dock Street, Edgartown, sculptured by the snow.

an anchorage as the winding harbor of Edgartown, with its moonglade reaching across the water toward Cape Poge. Here, summer loitered, stood still, while all creation drank, inhaled, and wholly experienced a richly stored elixir compounded of full leaf, golden sunlight, and fantasies without earthly limit. If, as Shaler said, the long Vineyard spring had arrests that seemed retardations, the rather short Vineyard summers had arrests that seemed forever.

The Martha's Vineyard Camp Meeting, genesis of the present-day town of Oak Bluffs, was established in 1835. Revivalists had preached on the Vineyard for some years, among them the famous "Reformation John" Adams who, upon leaving his flock, wrote:

> At Holmes' Hole there's some grown cold
> Oh Lord revive them down the Neck;
> The harbor round with blessings crown,
> With power the devil's kingdom shake!

Revival meetings seem to realize their most natural expression out of doors, in tents, under summer suns, and in the encouragement of soft breezes. Jeremiah Pease of Edgartown went exploring to find a proper meeting place, and he came upon it in a grove of oaks near the shore of Squash Meadow Pond, which was destined to become Oak Bluffs harbor. Well away from all worldliness, the grove was seven and a half miles distant from Edgartown over a winding, hilly dirt road, and between five and six miles from Holmes Hole. There was a closer approach across the harbor, only two miles if a road were to be built along the barrier beach that, except for a narrow opening, closed the Lagoon.

In Wesleyan Grove, as Jeremiah Pease first found it, the stand of oaks represented an ideal remoteness. Nature, undefiled and unalloyed, overflowed with sensuous wiles. How could there have been a sweeter place? Here the evangelical spirit could swell as strongly and as frequently as the tides from the sea. In August 1835 the first tents were pitched and a lectern built of driftwood.

Summer after summer, church groups from such places as New Bedford, Fairhaven, Fall River, Nantucket, and Providence attended the meetings, their delegations quartered in "society tents" arranged in a half circle. A partition separated men from women, and all slept on fresh straw or hay laid on the ground. In time, family tents were established in a circle set back from the society tents, in greater numbers every August. During the meeting of 1855 there were some two hundred tents, of which a hundred and fifty were supplied by "brethren wishing to be more domestic in their household affairs, and to enjoy retreat from the crowd, at least part of the time."

In 1859 William B. Lawton of Providence had a cottage ornamented with jigsaw filigree along the eaves built at Warren, Rhode Island, and shipped it to Wesleyan Grove to replace his family tent. Some tents already had wooden floors or frames; and the transition to fancy cottages, once begun, continued steadily. In a few years Edgartown contractors were taking orders for cottages by the dozen, all of them decorated with jigsaw scrollwork, gables of curious design, turrets, spires, and miniature balconies. Gothic doors and windows gave an ecclesiastical accent, but a holiday spirit could not be suppressed. Croquet was allowed, though not during Camp Meeting Week. The fashionable crinolines, stovepipe hats, sunbonnets, walking sticks, and sunshades impressed visitors. One of them called the meeting a "monster tented tea party."

Leasing privileges for good campground locations were held at a premium; yet at the perimeter of the grove there were open lands, part of what was once called the Great Pasture, reaching to the bluffs and to Vineyard Sound itself. Before the close of the 1868 meeting, most of this seventy-five-acre tract had been acquired by a new enterprise, the Oak Bluffs Land and Wharf Company, the Vineyard's first thrust into land development and speculation. Edgartown sea captains provided most of the capital, and the promotional leadership was supplied by the Honorable Erastus P. Carpenter of Foxboro, who was impressed with the opportunities for profit.

It was no longer necessary to drive or walk from the landings at Eastville to the campground and the new resort; the remoteness prized by Jeremiah Pease had disappeared. A new beach road shortened the distance from Edgartown, and the Lagoon bridge spanned the gap in the beach road from Vineyard Haven. The Edgartown captains dug deeper into their capital to construct, with the help of the town and the mainland Old Colony Railroad, a narrow-gauge railroad along the beach from the new Oak Bluffs to Edgartown, and on to the spectacular surf of South Beach.

Rushed to completion, the railroad began operation in August 1874, at the last gasp of the season; but not before the first locomotive had been rejected because it wouldn't take a curve, and the second, the "Active," had been catapulted from a flatcar into the water at the end of the Woods Hole dock. The season was redeemed at last in late August when President Ulysses

Above: Cottages in Oak Bluffs. Below: Elegant fashions of the past displayed in the attic of the Dukes County Historical Society museum.

Above: Enjoying the Illumination. Below: Community singing in the Tabernacle.

S. Grant stepped from the steamer *River Queen* at the Camp Meeting wharf and was whisked away to the campground in a magnificently decorated horsecar.

These were the great days both of the Oak Bluffs Company and the Camp Meeting. The Oak Bluffs promoters were openhanded; they built the Sea View Hotel at the head of their wharf, a chapel, and miles of streets, and provided many parks.

In 1877, in one of the first references to what has become a traditional Oak Bluffs festival, the Illumination, a visiting journalist wrote: "And still the view is more curious in the evening when every cottage is lighted, and the wide front doors, which open directly into the principal room, are thrown wide open, and the cottagers are sitting around inside or on the broad piazzas or balconies, and on gala evenings, when the fancy-colored Chinese lanterns are hung around on trees and cottages, the scene is really enchanting, as if Aladdin's lamp had transported one to fairyland."

No one knows just when or how the Illumination was adopted as a Camp Ground observance. There was an early rule that a lantern be kept lighted in each tent every night, and an observer then had written: "The tents and cottages dimly lighted by a single lamp in each may be imagined to resemble the celestial city's pearly gates, whose translucence would manifest the beauty of the glorious light within." But when the Oak Bluffs Company sponsored an Illumination in the summer of 1869, the display glowed with a new effulgence.

Lights were everywhere, in cottage windows, along the shore of the lake, in the parks, and borne by paraders marching to the music of the Foxboro Brass Band. Chinese and Japanese lanterns provided the most festive illumination. In succeeding years, different regions of the Camp Ground became friendly rivals: one tree-shaded avenue was christened Happy Valley and displayed a banner announcing THE VINEYARD IS OUR RESTING PLACE, HEAVEN IS OUR HOME. After the decline of the Oak Bluffs Company, other groups continued the Illuminations, and today they are still a summer event.

As the cottages replaced tents, an iron tabernacle, supported by arches of almost incredible delicacy, replaced the canvas tabernacle under which President Grant had sat and, tradition says, had been moved to profess his adherence to righteousness until deterred by the advice of his attorney general.

In retrospect, one could see how the great resurgence of religion following the Civil War had carried the Camp Meeting to the popularity of which

Hebron Vincent boasted: "The place is, indeed, unique; the progress has been wonderful; and the gatherings here, consisting as they do of people and clergymen from different parts of the country, are quite 'national.' "

The Oak Bluffs Company, though, had run its course. Its magnificent Sea View Hotel was destroyed by a fire that also took a huge skating rink. The latter was replaced by a later rink where Andrew D. White, scholar and diplomat, was astonished to find skaters whirling around the floor to the tune of "Nearer My God to Thee." But nothing like the Sea View was built again.

The tracks of the railroad along the beach were repeatedly washed out by winter storms, at a ruinous annual expense, and the line failed. Many another land scheme launched in the boom years also failed, and in a surprisingly brief time the stakes marking ambitiously proposed streets, parks, and avenues were lost in wild growth, and a toboggan slide went the way of other recreational enterprises.

Victim of overconfidence and overexpansion, the Oak Bluffs Company slowly died, but not without leaving a new town as its legacy. Before the end, the promoters tried to recoup as well as they could, first by selling their wharf to the Old Colony Railroad, then purveying as building lots the parks which, they now claimed, they had retained under their ownership.

This precipitated an historic Cottage City Park Case decision by Justice Oliver Wendell Holmes, then of the Supreme Judicial Court of Massachusetts, who ruled that the public had accepted the parks through usage and enjoyment and that no other formality was necessary.

The seven-foot picket fence built by the Camp Meeting Association to exclude the exuberant worldliness of Oak Bluffs was reduced in height, then most of it was removed. Soon there was agitation to separate both Camp Ground and Oak Bluffs from the parent Edgartown, to create a new township. The first baby born within the campground, symbolically named Wesley Grove Vincent, arrived in December 1871 and later became a distinguished surgeon.

The new town won its independence after a bitter struggle of several years and was named Cottage City, for the resort had been advertised in railroad literature as the Cottage City of America. The name "Oak Bluffs" was still tainted with the unpopularity of the Edgartown promoters. But by 1907 the name "Cottage City" was deemed inelegant, and a petition induced the legislature to change it to Oak Bluffs.

Despite the failure of the land companies and the stresses of the depression of the late seventies, the Cottage City of America reached a new crest of

Sunday evening concert in Ocean Park.

popularity in the nineties. At Cottage City the nineties were indeed gay; the resort seemed to have been created for that cheerful decade. A band played in Ocean Park and saluted arriving visitors; the beaches were crowded with oddly costumed men, women, and children; bicyclists, sporting tight pants, blazers, and visored caps, came in groups and held parades of their own.

Summer days were lived outdoors on cottage porches, under trees, and along Circuit Avenue, where the decorative jigsaw scrollwork of shops and hotels might be admired, and curios that later generations would discard as stuffy could be purchased to grace the parlors at home.

Other influences on the growth of Oak Bluffs proved more lasting than the fads of the nineties. When the Camp Meeting Association felt pressed by the tide of enterprise and recreation, the Vineyard Grove Company was formed to acquire and preserve fifty-five acres on the northerly side of Lake Anthony, the expansively renamed Squash Meadow Pond. Ironically, this protective group later became a land-development enterprise. Meantime, however, the Methodists remained in their original campground, and a Baptist Vineyard Association built a temple and held camp meetings among the oaks "over Jordan" on the far side of Lake Anthony. Here, in the Vineyard Highlands, the Martha's Vineyard Summer Institute was later founded. The Highland wharf was soon known as the Baptist Landing. Disembarking passengers could reach the original campground by horse car.

The varied contours of the Highlands extend across the promontory of East Chop, from Oak Bluffs to Eastville, commanding a magnificent view of Vineyard Sound and Vineyard Haven harbor from what was once Ebenezer Smith's sheep pasture. A historian of 1908 wrote: "at our feet is . . . an enchantment of opalescent color, of white caps and doldrums, of catboats and steamers and tows and schooners, and across the five miles of water the scattering villages of the Cape."

The steamers and schooners are long gone, but the running tides and still-nesses of the Sound remain; often the summer sun strikes down upon an unforgettable expanse of blue and white and green, in timeless moments of beauty that seem suspended in eternity. An evening breeze rises, the Sound murmurs at the foot of the bluffs, the empty sail of some small knockabout offshore fills again, and motion is resumed.

If the piping of the pinkletinks may be taken as the voice of an island spring, the scent of the sweet pepper bush may be taken as the unspoken message of an island August. There are many other summer fragrances, such as that of the swamp honeysuckle of July, which carry far, but the sweet

Autumn shadows in
the Camp Ground.

Above: Cycling in the hills. Below: Cattle grazing in the fertile meadows.

pepper bush is a superb conqueror of distances. Its essence spreads and intensifies in the langorous evening air, after the sun has subsided in the low sky opposite the cliffs of Gay Head.

This tall bush, *Clethra alnifolia,* flourishes in all swampy places, so that no single region alone possesses it; yet it is particularly identified with upisland areas, from West Tisbury westward to Gay Head itself. The "pepper" in the name derives from the small brownish dots carried on the racemes of the creamy flowers.

Following this August scent upisland, one soon comes to West Tisbury and the serenely beautiful inland valley of the Old Mill River wandering down to the Mill Pond and then on again into Tisbury Great Pond. Some maps justly designate the river as a brook, but the memory of ancient mill sites, its relative size and dignity among Vineyard brooks, and the authority of tradition entitle it to be called a river. Its tributaries rise in the Indian Hill country to the north and in the hills to the west, joining at North Tisbury.

The inland valley, so old and wise in fertility, seems to hold summer as its own. Somerset Maugham, visiting Martha's Vineyard, was reminded of Devonshire. And similar comparisons have been made by many travelers. At the edge of the outwash plain, where the roads climb with many intervals of descent into the hills of Chilmark and Gay Head, is West Tisbury. To all appearances, it might be far from the sea; yet it hears the beat of the surf, and its roads lead soon to the coves which once provided a distinctive way of life for the Great Pond folk. Wild fowl, eels, shellfish, and two or three cuttings of salt hay from marshes that reach toward the ocean marked a succession of productivity the year around. The Great Pond people needed little else, except their heirloom tools and a few things, like molasses, bought at the town's general store. And among the coves of the great ponds of West Tisbury and Chilmark, in the hills and on the moors, there were great flocks of sheep.

When the British fleet entered Holmes Hole harbor in September 1778, Major General Gray raided the entire island for supplies; the fleet sailed again with ten thousand Vineyard sheep and some three hundred oxen. Those great flocks of the old years are gone, and few sheep are pastured in West Tisbury now; the pastures have returned to wild growth, and the "water fences" that extended across the beaches of the North Shore into the tidewater to keep sheep in their own preserves have disappeared.

West Tisbury, they say, has in its summer bounty every type of wildflower found in Massachusetts. The village has been called both a sermon and a

38

poem; its dewy aspect on a July or August morning is both delight and re-assurance.

Here is an old-fashioned, prodigal garden by the roadside, an oasis of color where flowers grow with a will; atop a neighboring barn an old-fashioned but forever-young horse on the windvane gallops eternally out of the past into the present.

The old mill and mill pond, though somnolent now, the placid home of swans, tell of past enterprise. There were many mill sites on the Old Mill River; in some meal and corn were ground, and in this one, now the Martha's Vineyard Garden Club Center, cloth was made of island wool. Whalemen wore garments of this homely manufacture on long voyages in the Pacific.

The road goes past the mill and around a bluff still known as Brandy Brow, though the origin of the name is vague; the belief is that a dram shop once stood here, though the terrain would seem particularly unsuitable. Near by is Parsonage Pond and, looking down upon it, an old, old house with small diamond-shaped windowpanes. The house is one of the unmistakable symbols of the town; it has been, since 1840, the Whiting place. It stands upon part of the homestead lot of Josiah Standish, son of Captain Miles Standish; and not far distant, on Scotchman's Bridge Lane, is the Betty Alden place, completing the poetic association.

In West Tisbury nothing is out of tune, from the brooding Agricultural Hall, to the three-story, mansard-roofed Currier & Ives schoolhouse, the steepled white church, and the boundary bridge across the Tiasquin River, where the town yields to Chilmark. Well-shaded Music Street sedately wears its pride of culture: schoolhouse, library, church, and the memory of seven pianos purchased for the daughters of seven families in prompt emulation of the style set by Captain George A. Smith. Not only their music, but also that of the many birds, the winds—smoky sou'westers and blustery no'theasters—the distant surf beat, the cicadas of August, and the perfect insect symphony of September, all belong to West Tisbury.

"Loveliest village of the plain" but not deserted yet, nor will it ever be, West Tisbury bears the impress of all the island generations, as clearly visible as the morainal relics of the glacier. Unbroken for some three centuries, the love and labor of island husbandry has come down to us in homes thriftily built, fields fenced and tilled, amid a self-sufficiency of earth, brook, pond, and sea. If sunlight is ever eternal, if wildflowers have any security of dominion, West Tisbury is one of the earth's chosen spots.

Within West Tisbury Township is Lambert's Cove, a gently curving inden-

Below: The First Congregational Church, West Tisbury. Overleaf: Skaters on Parsonage Pond.

tation from Vineyard Sound, with Makonikey Bluffs on the east, Paul's Point on the west. The region is rough and hilly, with half-ridden winding pathways, stone walls that climb high slopes only to dip again, and blue flecks of ponds. Near the shore is James Pond, bearing out John Brereton's description of a great standing lake of fresh water.

Inland from the cove is the first Indian Hill; its summit was the dancing field of the Indians. A better-known hill of the same name was adopted and christened by livery-stable drivers in early resort days because it was more easily reached; it, too, was authentically an Indian Hill, with a few fieldstone graves upon one slope. The first Indian Hill is upward and shoreward from wooded Christiantown, now quiet and deserted, the last of its Indian residents gone for some forty years. At one time the population numbered sixty, and there may have been more at the time the sachem, Josias, "gave one square mile of land unto my uncle, Pamick Nonoussa, Tachquanum & Poxsin of Taukemey to be a township for them," setting a site for the home village of the "Praying Indians." A gray shingled chapel stands by the road, opposite the Christiantown cemetery.

The chapel and burying ground are in the center of a sanctuary safeguarded by the county ownership and are enriched by wildflower plantings and inviting trails through the adjacent woods.

Both Indian Hills are among a group of four that rise more than two hundred feet above the sea. From either, at the turn of the century and for at least a decade after, one could always see a fleet of coasters in Vineyard Sound; and from the first Indian Hill, one could also see the Lambert's Cove meetinghouse, "perched on the top of a slight elevation and lifting its proud head above the surrounding woods," so an exploring minister described it.

Three main roads take the traveler upisland; the oldest, South Road, was first dirt, then white macadam, and long afterward acquired a modern blacktop. This road could have run directly from Vineyard Haven across the edge of the plain to West Tisbury, but state highway builders chose their route in a swing northward in order to pass through Middletown, where the North Tisbury post office stood until 1914, when Rural Free Delivery came to the island. Middletown spread its church and houses along the road and in outskirt fields and byways, as it does today, and for many years the West Tisbury town hall occupied what is now the fire station.

North Tisbury is the junction of the North and South Roads, but the Middle Road begins at Baxter's Corner, the terminus of Music Street, unless one includes a cutoff called the Panhandle, which crosses the level fields.

Mayhew Chapel, Christiantown.

An Indian Hill cemetery.

A Chilmark vista.

By these three roads one comes upon three quite different parts of Chilmark. Since Chilmark reaches from shore to shore of an island whose inhabitants pridefully refer to it as a continent in miniature, the existence of differences is easily understood. As a matter of fact, the town has an almost continuous water border of ponds to the west, as Vineyarders were once forcibly reminded when a hurricane swept out the road and bridge which connect Chilmark and Gay Head.

The ocean on one side and Vineyard Sound on the other give Chilmark wide margins, but much of the spaciousness is overhead; the Chilmark hills reach up, if not in terms of absolute altitude, then all the more impressively in their proportionate triumph over lower levels. The farmer here could rest on his hoe and view the Atlantic, and if it were not for the curvature of the earth and the sea mist he might see North Africa.

An obstinate man on the mainland whose wife had gone to Chilmark sued for divorce on the ground that she had put "an oceanic body of water" between them. This may have been a lawyer-like exaggeration, but Chilmark has looked up, around, and widely all about, since the Mayhews, Bassetts, Tiltons, Vincents, and Flanderses first took possession.

From the South Road as it curves and mounts into Chilmark there are sweeping vistas across moors and ravines to the ocean, beyond a great pond and the barrier beach. The North Road leads to intimacy with an inland valley, and the Middle Road, still deeper inland, follows a course through the hills until it joins the South Road again at Beetlebung Corner.

Beetlebung Corner? Strangers invariably ask about the name. Here, an easy stone's throw backward along the South Road from the intersection of South, Middle, and Menemsha Crossroads, is a grove of tupelo or black gum trees—*Nyssa sylvatica*—not far from the town hall, general store, schoolhouse, community center, and bank. The branches reach out in uncompromising straightness, giving the tree a stanchly individual appearance. In the fall its rather small leaves blaze with every conceivable shade of red, in tune with the sumacs, swamp maples, and the thickets of huckleberry on the hills. The wood of the tupelo is heavy, cross-grained as a farmer in a tantrum, soft, and hard to work. It was used to make a ramming instrument known as a beetle, close relative of the bung starter. The tree has taken on the name of the instrument made from it, and in turn graciously lent it to the crossroads corner.

Before the Middle Road reaches Beetlebung Corner, it pursues a pleasant course through the valley, passes over the Tiasquin River, meets Tea Lane,

Overleaf: Chilmark Pond.

45

and crosses Fulling Mill Brook, coming at last to a height from which, unexpectedly and completely, the companionship of trees, hills, and stone walls gives way to a broad view across green farmsteads and countryside to the Atlantic.

Chilmark has hills meant for long views, for exultation, and for summer thought and philosophy, dips and valleys for concealment, and swamps for moisture. Great ponds are held within barrier beaches along the ocean shore and in the elbow of Squibnocket Point. The beach on any summer day appears white and peaceful, but with wind and tide the sands conspire to move; they are seldom really still. They may be driven inland, they heap and level off, all at the caprice of weather; but mostly their course is from west to east, urged on by slanting surf and prevailing southwest winds.

High above both beach and sea are the cliffs of Wequobsque, and between pond and ocean the wind-carved dunes of Squibnocket resound with the unceasing roll of surf upon white sand.

Among the Chilmark hills are New Boston, with its magnificent panorama; Mosher's; Abel's; and Great House Hill; little-known Alice's Hill; and Whale Hill, where long ago watch was kept for offshore whales. Blue and white violets grow in profusion on Violet Hill, and Money Hill may be the site of lost and buried treasure.

Beyond Squibnocket are Lookout, called Panorama Hill by the summer people, and Pine Tree, Powwow, Elijah's, and Shot-an-Arrow. From Creek Hill above Menemsha both Newport and New Bedford may be seen on a clear day. Down the North Road is Prospect, 308 feet high, the Vineyard's loftiest summit since the Army shaved off a few feet of Peaked Hill. Little Peaked, Bassett's Hill, and Sugar Loaf may all be seen from the North Road. Bassett's Hill was once the site of the town hall, then known as Woodpecker Hall because of the attention the flickers bestowed upon it.

The hills and their scattering of boulders are, of course, relics of the last of the glaciers; but in Chilmark, Barbara Blau Chamberlain says, you can dig down through time. In some places only a scant top covering was glacier-borne; beneath are preglacial materials pushed ahead and raised up by the ice front in the manner of a great bulldozer.

Crèvecoeur in 1762 wrote that "Chilmark contains stone for fencing." Mrs. Chamberlain places immediate responsibility upon the Buzzards Bay lobe of the glacier which "blanketed all with its till. Frequently the ridges tore loose boulders from the lobe's lower surface, creating boulder concentrations in the till. Nearly everywhere stones are abundant. They range from mere pebbles up to twenty-five-foot blocks of granite, clumped in piles, as one geologist described, like 'ruined Cyclopean masonry' or simply strewn across the surface."

In the middle of the nineteenth century Chilmark was crosshatched by some forty miles of stone walls that surmounted the hills and were silhouetted against the sky, looking "like the fancy filament of a queen's crown" and adding not a little to the landscape. Many of the walls are now deep in the woods where old pastures have been overgrown since the decline of sheep grazing and extensive agriculture. Some walls have been ground up for road-building or built into the foundations of houses.

Squibnocket Pond, some say, was once a harbor. The Indian name means "where the red groundnut grows," in allusion to the bulb of the red lily. The Indians, Dr. Banks, the island historian, says, ate the roots, "which are long in the boiling and taste like the liver of sheep."

Menemsha has a fame which has grown with the years, depending on the importance of fishing village, creek, pond, and bight. Menemsha Pond had once been an arm of the sea, and in the later decades of the nineteenth century there was agitation to reopen it. A creek was dredged in 1903, jetties were constructed to protect the opening, the pond became a safe anchorage for small craft, and the channel and basin of Menemsha became a seaport.

It became much more; succeeding to the traditions of Gulltown on Noman's Land and of Lobsterville on the Gay Head shore of Menemsha Bight without departing from its own function and character, it became a busy fishing village which has survived decades of vacationers, artists, and, lately, even sightseeing busses. Yet the essential Menemsha is there, unpretentious, practical, unchanged.

The hurricane of 1938 brought a huge torrent from the Atlantic through the ponds and across the island, sweeping away most of the old Menemsha, but the new village reproduces the old almost as if nothing had happened.

New docks have been built, and new houses on Creek Hill and Chowder Kettle Lane; new faces appear among the fishermen whose family names are so often the same as those who once set trap gear in Vineyard Sound or went lobstering in boats long before the era of marine engines. Menemsha, old and new, reaches back from its bulkheads, beaches, and jetties into a countryside of hills and ravines where beach plums and huckleberries ripen, wildflowers follow the seasons, and the blaze of autumn runs alongside the deep blue and cresting white of Vineyard Sound.

Overleaf: Menemsha in the hurricane of 1938.

49

Gay Head, the compellingly beautiful western headland of Martha's Vineyard with its cliffs of many-colored clay, has a geological record measured not in thousands but in millions of years. Fossils of whales, camels, and elephants have been found, and Barbara Blau Chamberlain says that some of the lignite in the cliffs is "a hundred-million-year-old plant tomb in which pieces of ancient tree trunks, still recognizable, lie with reddish-yellow drops of an amber-like material which may be gum from the nuts of the eucalyptus tree."

One of those rare, glassy objects known as tektites, picked up at Gay Head, adds cosmic distance to cosmic age; it may have come from the moon. Scientists do not all agree, but they have estimated the age of this specimen at 33,600,000 years.

Once Gay Head gave life to magnolias, sequoias, and eucalyptus, but now only oaks, pines, willows, hollies, and sassafras remain. Legend says that the first visitors here were Indians who arrived on ice cakes, but even as a legend it does not speak with confidence.

Moshup, Gay Head's own legendary chief and giant, must have been very early on the scene, for he dealt in forces as mighty as those of nature herself. With the emptying of ashes from his pipe he created Nantucket; and the great boulders, mostly submerged, which reach out into Vineyard Sound from Gay Head, were part of his causeway to Cuttyhunk. Though he was not a devil, except perhaps in a special sense, the boulders are known as Devil's Bridge and upon them, in 1884, the steamer *City of Columbus* was wrecked on a bitter January night with the loss of seventy-five passengers and twenty-eight officers and members of the crew.

Moshup and Old Squant and the squaw who used to be seen walking across the moors carrying her head in her hands must be accorded an appropriate Gay Head residential priority. But one of the earliest visitors may have been Leif Ericson, son of Eric the Red, hero of the sagas, and his shelter or booth may have been erected on Noman's Land, four miles at sea from Gay Head. Or was the Vineyard itself the Straumey, or Island of Tides, described by the Norsemen; and did they not build the cromlech of Nashaquitsa?

The earliest written reference to Gay Head is that of Gabriel Archer, one of the two chroniclers of Bartholomew Gosnold's voyage, in 1602: "The four-and-twentieth, we set sail and doubled the Cape of another Island . . . which we called Dover Cliff." Geologically, the cliffs of Dover and those of Gay Head are cousins, as the crew of the *Concord* immediately recognized.

The setting sun brings out the full glory and variety of the Gay Head

Opposite: After the hurricane and restoration, Menemsha returned to its usual tranquillity.

53

escarpment with its lofty projections, falls, and profiles, inviting colorful description. Daniel Webster wrote in 1849: "Gay Head is what Niagara would be if instead of 150 feet of falling water, it exhibited a perpendicular bank of that height, composed of lines, strata, and sections of various earths and highly contrasted colors. . . . In the afternoon sun, and especially when recently washed by rain, the appearance is splendid and gorgeous."

Early in October 1852 the Reverend Robert McGonegal, pastor of the Chilmark church, counted twenty-five different colors in the cliffs of Gay Head. "Stand with me, if you will," he wrote, "upon the extreme point of a bluff or headland which runs out to the very brink of the sea—150 feet, almost perpendicular above the water—stand still; the least careless movement might precipitate you to destruction. Look now at the glorious orb of day just rolling himself down the western horizon, hiding half his golden rays partially behind a fleecy cloud which rests like a thin mantle upon the bank where he seeks repose for the coming night."

The Reverend Mr. McGonegal was overly nervous about the risk of falling down the cliffs, and overly poetic in his style; but all the same the autumn months, perhaps October particularly, bring the clearest air and the most spectacular and enduring afterglows of the island year.

Many have recorded their impressions of the magnificent spectacle of Gay Head, but the record at once most accurate, most imaginative, and most enduringly satisfactory is the photographic one. It dramatically emphasizes the continuing tragedy of the cliffs: the erosion by the elements which may one day reduce them to nothing, and the vandalism which yearly eats into and defaces the profiles and hollows.

Stewart C. Udall, as Secretary of the Interior, recognizing their magnificence and dignity, declared the cliffs a National Monument. And Army engineers have been authorized to make a survey to determine what methods will control the tragic erosion.

At one time the lighthouse, the Magic Lantern of Gay Head, was almost as much an attraction as the cliffs, even though an expedition from Edgartown or Vineyard Haven to Gay Head was painfully slow, across many sandy hills with some thirty pairs of pasture bars which had to be taken down and replaced. Daniel Webster found the long drive fatiguing. Many visitors made two days of the journey, staying overnight in the hospitable home of the lightkeeper.

The greatest fame of the lighthouse lamps followed the installation of the most ambitious lens of Augustin Jean Fresnel, an attraction which had been

The Gay Head cliffs drop
dramatically to the sea.

Seal basking on Moshup's causeway.

exhibited at the London World's Fair in 1851 and purchased by the United States Government for sixteen thousand dollars.

A year after the lens was installed General David Hunter Strother wrote in *Harper's* magazine: "Of all the heavenly phenomena that I have had the good fortune to witness—borealis lights, mock suns or meteoric showers—I have never seen anything that, in mystic splendor, equalled this trick of the magic lantern of Gay Head."

The Gay Head Light, of course, was eventually converted to electricity and the keeper replaced by automation. The famous Fresnel lens, now dispensable, was coveted by a mainland museum, but the Dukes County Historical Society has saved it for the island and it is installed in a tower on the society's grounds at Edgartown.

The sea, the lighthouse, and the Coast Guard station which was erected atop the cliffs following the 1884 *City of Columbus* disaster dominated life in the peninsula community. Susan Goldin Heinz, whose father was light-keeper, has written of her childhood in Gay Head:

"In September 1937 I entered the first grade of the Gay Head School, that one-roomed, pond-side, flagpole-headed building watched over by two outhouses. They were a brisk winter's run from the coal-warmed inside, not so far as to get a chill, but far enough to lose the warm gray air from my long blond curls and from the thick, black braids of my two best friends. . . .

"Our one-room schoolhouse was not red. . . . It was gray, bleached by salt spray scattered over the moors of Gay Head by the ocean which drew up our lives close around us, the better to see the broad neck of land on which we lived. . . .

"Recess was always welcome but never more so than during winter months when the pond beside the school froze over. We were all poor by city standards, but we had ice skates and a lot of time to use them. . . . Some days I would roller skate the mile and a half home to my lighthouse, the one my parents operated, perched at the top of the Gay Head cliffs.

"Long stretches of beach and strands and faint rumbles of distant waves that crashed the land and washed my eyes with beauty that sand could never swallow. Tall grass that dried brown in early fall. . . . What sifts over time, from any years, perhaps, is what goes on inside, those moments when you put something inside yourself and make it yours. You run with the wind to blow spume over the dunes. You pull pine needles from your tangled hair and smarting scalp. You have lived with the ocean so long and loved it so well that you can close your eyes any time and see the waves breaking, hear

The Coast Guard station.

Mr. and Mrs. Napoleon Madison exemplify the Indian heritage of Gay head.

them, feel the taste of spray on your lips, in your eyes. You remember the sting of wind and slowly feel what a friend has felt, and why.

"Experience is such a personal thing, but that is how it was at Gay Head for me."

The lighthouse dominates the landscape at Gay Head, but it is the Indians who traditionally hold the principal role in the life of the community. History tells how Thomas Mayhew traveled to Gay Head from Edgartown on Sunday to deliver two-hour sermons to them; how Indian militia drilled at Gay Head during King Philip's war of extermination, despite the excited fears of the mainland; how Gay Head was administered largely by the Society for the Propagation of the Gospel in New England, and after a long evolution became a township in 1870; and how Edwin D. Vanderhoop of Gay Head became the first Indian to take a seat in the House of Representatives in Massachusetts.

The Gay Head Indians were and are fishermen, and their prowess in whaling was in demand well into this century. Joseph G. Belain, who died in the nineteen twenties at the age of seventy-nine, had spent sixty years on whaleships; and Amos Smalley, who died more recently, was the only man known to have harpooned a white whale.

In the eighties, when overland journeys over sandy roads were arduous, steamboat excursions to Gay Head were popular. Colored handbills were scattered in the larger Cape Cod and island towns advertising trips through Vineyard Sound to the clay cliffs.

"Three hours to explore this world-renowned headland of Martha's Vineyard and inspect the magnificent light with its wonderful mechanism," the broadside urged. "Take your knife and paper box along and cut out some of the variegated clay." A wharf was built below the cliffs, and an oxcart—described in the handbills as "a Gay Head omnibus, driven by a Native Indian"—carried excursionists to the summit. Sometimes the voyages were made by moonlight, with a brass band aboard the side-wheel steamer.

Gay Head today, still at heart and in spirit an Indian town, raises more immediately and urgently than any other region of Martha's Vineyard the question of values, those of nature and of culture, tradition, and the significance of the island to those who know it or who may seek it out. As the famous cliffs recede, human resources and values also recede.

The passing of the glaciers produced in Martha's Vineyard an entity which impresses visitors in different ways. Nathaniel Shaler expressed his apprecia-

John Mayhew, like his kinsman Thomas, shared in a family tradition that has given many ministers of the gospel to Martha's Vineyard.

The beauty of the sea.

tion of another aspect of its beauty: "Water in all its phases is at its best on Martha's Vineyard. The Vineyard Sound on the North Shore gives the perfection of quiet-water bathing. It is warm enough to tempt and hold the lovers of sea bathing; warm enough to require more courage to leave than to enter it. The faint swing it has, for it is not altogether still, is as soothing as a cradle's rocking. If this be too tame for the sturdy bather, he has only to cross the Island to the South Shore to find another face on the sea. The long shore, straight as if drawn by a rule for fifteen miles or more—stands in the middle and it runs to the horizon as straight as a prairie railway—is beaten by the surges which can roll directly down upon it from six thousand miles of water. . . . The great waves roll with solemn regularity upon the shore; they are never still. . . . Nowhere is the calm so great as this half imprisonment by the sea."

There's the sea, not always gentle in the Sound nor boisterous in the Atlantic, and there's the wind; and the famous wind for sailing is the sou'-wester. In *The Bay and the Sound* the yachtsman John Parkinson, Jr., wrote: "Probably the most pleasant places to wrestle with sou'westers are the lee shores of Martha's Vineyard and the Nantucket islands, whose protective bluffs provide comparatively smooth water over a wide area. No wonder Vineyard Haven, Edgartown, and Nantucket are so popular with so many yachtsmen. For there is nothing more exciting than to be well up in a big fleet of cruiser-racers, beating for the finish line in a hard sou'wester off Edgartown. It is usually a very long leg, the sea is very smooth, and the yachts are practically up to hull speed. Puffs come off the shore even harder as the line draws closer—gusts that can knock a boat right down to the cabin house."

"Practically up to hull speed"—there's the excitement. Sailors from Scandinavia and other maritime countries, contestants in the Soling Class eastern championships in August 1969, were astonished at the Edgartown winds.

Others have written of the safe harbors; or, looking inland, of the moors, hills, ponds, and wooded places.

Descriptions of Martha's Vineyard are rarely objective; the beauty implicit in shore, sea, wind, and moor has always inspired the beholder. Unfortunately, in the long perspective, there has been diminution of resources to an extent few moderns realize. John Brereton's account of "high-timbered oaks, their leaves thrice so broad as ours; cedars, tall and straight; beech, elm, holly, walnut trees in abundance . . . hazelnut trees, cherry trees . . . sassafras trees in great plenty all the island over . . . also divers other fruit trees," must scarcely be conceivable to motorists who drive across the scrub oak plain between Edgartown and West Tisbury today. Shaler estimated in 1888 that plowing and forest fires—forest fires mostly—had rendered 33,000 acres untillable. The trees now growing in the State Forest on the plain demonstrate that most of this region can be replenished; but the incentive is small, other prospects are brighter, and patience is a virtue long outmoded.

The erosion of the shores is another concern. Older inhabitants, and now their children and grandchildren, tell how a succession of ponds along the South Shore once made it possible to skate from Edgartown to Squibnocket with few overland treks; the beach has been eaten back, small ponds have disappeared. In the first three decades of this century much of the island's ocean beach was fortified by massive dunes largely stabilized by beach grass and other hardy growth. Then the great hurricane of 1938 leveled the dunes so that flattened beaches lay vulnerable to surf and wind, but perhaps the forces that built the old dunes may slowly take charge again. In the early thirties a world-wide disease caused the eel grass which lay in extensive underwater meadows in the quieter waters around the island to disappear completely. With the stabilizing eel grass gone, changes in the shore line—erosion here, shoaling there—took place rapidly. Now, after more than thirty years, the eel grass is back.

The great enemy, of course, is not nature but man—man's haste, indifference, ignorance, laziness, and greed. The Vineyard's insularity was preserved from most of the ugliness and pressure of civilization until after World War II. Now there are no islands any more—and this is as anxiously true in the South Seas as off the heel of Cape Cod.

The values of Martha's Vineyard, and of other places like it, though recognized and vital, will not survive unless they are fought for. Fortunately, major strides have been made in the past few years toward preservation, as sanctuaries, of characteristic regions in different parts of the island: Cedar Tree Neck, with its pond, its headland extending into Vineyard Sound, and some two hundred hinterland acres of woodland and swamp descending in glacial terrain from the North Shore ridge to the wash of Vineyard Sound; Felix Neck in Sengekontacket Pond, with two hundred acres of woods, old farmland, salt marsh, and pond shore, title to which will be held by the Massachusetts Audubon Society; and a series of assertively individual domains, each district in character, to be owned and administered by the Trustee of Reservations, a long-established corporation with successfully

Giant oak in North Tisbury. Overleaf: Winter winds whip the shore between Oak Bluffs and Edgartown.

Above: Bird watchers at Tisbury Great Pond. Below: Scalloping at Chilmark.

managed open spaces in many parts of Massachusetts. These are the Menemsha Hills, with more than two hundred acres of morainal hills and declivities and a mile of Sound shore; Cape Poge beach on Chappaquiddick and the lonely land's end of beautiful Wasque Point; Little Neck, near Cape Poge, which is all salt marsh, shore, lean and scrubby thicket, a nesting place for sea and shore birds; and the former Tisbury Pond Club tract in the South Shore and Great Pond region of West Tisbury—all have been set aside within the past few years, most of them since 1967.

And there are others. The Sheriff's Meadow Foundation, which is responsible for the Cedar Tree Neck area of the Obed Sherman Daggett and Maria Roberts Daggett Sanctuary and the adjoining Alexander S. Reed Bird Refuge, is also preserving Sheriff's Meadow Pond and its surroundings in Edgartown, a hill and a small pond in North Tisbury, a sixty-acre native tract in the Middle Road territory. In all these there should be a secure and varied heritage extending the spirit of an island alive and all itself, and interpreting to the public a real present as well as a real past.

Chicory and Bouncing Bet bloom in August, both by the roadsides as if it were their purpose to be seen. Summer reaches out slowly toward fullness; the smoky sou'wester blows, and the shadows of trees and houses are as black as they will ever be. Goldenrod, the treasure that lies at the end of summer, begins to show itself early, and it will survive as an intermediary into the long fall, Indian summer, and the chill edge of winter.

Many who love the Vineyard associate the late summer and autumn changes with particular places. Some remember the ripening of wild apples along the Indian Hill Road, the reddening and bronzing of the huckleberry thickets on Chilmark hills, the scent of sweetfern at the edge of the road across the plain, or the first swamp-maple branch in spectacular red, orange, and yellow hues among the green near the ford at North Tisbury.

The grass in old meadows in West Tisbury turns ruddy, and if one searches with a little effort he will find there everlastings which, when dried, become "ladies' tobacco." Through the crisped leaves and thorny twigs of the wild rose the red rosehips are seen along all the paths, short cuts, and traveled ways. The berries of the black alder are thick in the hedgerows of the Middle Road. The wild grapes ripening, and the sweetness of their smell fills the air at Gay Head or in the swamps of the North Shore.

Crickets chirp and the temperature of a September or October night can be accurately told by the frequency of their chirping. From the darkness overheard a flying quawk drops its single syllable, and in the morning one hears the whickering of a flicker. The woods are washed with rain.

This is the time of the Milky Way and starlit sheen on the water, of white morning haze, of shrill red samphire along the rim of the Eel Pond at Edgartown—and other wet borders, too; and when the tupelos are changed into their own autumnal flame. The tupelo becomes, in the words of one aware botanist, "a pillar of fire indeed . . . only the reds of the swamp maples and sumacs compare with it in brilliancy." In this trinity—beetlebung, swamp maple, sumac—the Vineyard year maintains acute expression of its pageantry in fall.

No one can say for sure when Indian summer begins, and it may not end at all; its interludes may recur until they become gently changed into the unexpected days of early spring warmth when the sou'wester also blows.

But winter is seldom completely cheated. At first the white frosts, then the thinly roofed puddles in the morning, then the solid ice, the no'theasters, the lengthening of days and the strengthening of cold, according to the true old proverb and the meteorologists alike. Island temperatures are not so low as those of the mainland, but the driving winds can be bitter, the surf may thunder all day and all night against the South Beach. Occasional winters are almost completely open, but usually there is some snow, even if it yields quickly to a thaw, and there can be blizzards letting loose not only the violence but the grandeur of traditional New England winter storms.

When there is snow, the contours of the island seem to be freshly molded or sculptured; open to the sky, the wind, and the sun, they show themselves with something of the clarity of a three-dimensional photograph.

Bound from Woods Hole to the island, a winter traveler sees the profiles emphasized and accented; he sees the hills with their high slopes and shoulders boldly white, their crypts, falls, undulations marked out darkly. He can see where the hidden ponds and swamps are. His eye can bridge ravines and inland valleys, marking out their width and breadth; he sees the darkness of the evergreens and the nakedness of wind-slanted North Shore oaks; he picks out the indentations of the shore and the way the land rises in different manners from shore to hill. The bluffs of Makonikey are newly bold and candid; beyond is the ancient shelter of Lambert's Cove with Paul's Point beyond, and west of Paul's Point the island's farthest extension into Vineyard Sound, Cedar Tree Neck. Then far Cape Higgon—or Capigan or any of a dozen other forms of the name, its high bluffs descending to a point always with the same sweep and grace, whatever it is called. Menemsha Bight is

Above: The United Methodist Church, Chilmark. Overleaf: Menemsha Bight.

67

clearly seen, though Menemsha itself appears only as an indentation, with a spectacularly detailed Gay Head in long profile beyond.

The island ferries and steamers no longer go to and from Edgartown; they dock all year at Vineyard Haven and sometimes, in summer, at Oak Bluffs. But if the old side-wheeler *Uncatena* were still running, with the red-mustachioed Captain Marshall at her wheel, a passenger bound for Edgartown would be able to get his best view of the Chops, Vineyard Haven and its streets, towers, and rooftops rising on its hill, and the long, low island beach setting off Sengekontacket Pond from the Sound. He could see Cape Poge reaching out to sea, the bluffs of Chappaquiddick, and then at last the deep, winding harbor of Edgartown itself, and the landmarks of Chappaquiddick Point and Tower Hill.

Winter is a great artist, not only because of the forms and surfaces it produces with snow and ice, but in the precision with which it picks out, ornaments, and remakes so much that other seasons conceal or reduce to a kind of nothing-special background.

In the island towns the old life goes on: church suppers, town meetings, schools and school sports—so little different in essence from the life of the generations gone. Some—sociologists maybe—would make distinctions, stressing the basic changes modern technological advances have made; and the sociologists would be right. Drugstores now close at six instead of ten—for television has tolled the groups of bystanders and late-stayers into homes instead of stores. The downtown stores have no cast-iron stoves with elderly men sitting around, smoking, sometimes talking, sometimes keeping comfortable silence.

A time came when the older generation stayed home after supper and the younger generations, in new freedom, walked around downtown, stood on the corner in front of the drugstore or in the drugstore itself. Or, as views broadened and the automobile age evolved, the young people drove on the endless night errand of the young, arriving nowhere but home again at last.

Civilization has changed again, progressed, moved on, adopted the new patterns of convenience, settled into habits of its own age; and Martha's Vineyard is involved as all other places in this age and this civilization; yet it retains its flavor, purposes, character. Its basic challenges and decisions rest in the balance between man and nature, sea and shore, as in the time of the whaling captains. Modern yet not modern, ancient yet not ancient, the island's contradictions are themselves an elusive but genuine expression of an undefeated insularity.

The Four Corners, Edgartown.

70

Edgartown harbor.

Edgartown is still
a sailor's paradise.

Left: Bathing in the surf at Katama Beach. Above: The Harborside Inn pool commands a view of Chappaquiddick, with the Edgartown Yacht Club at the left.

Overleaf: Boat race, Edgartown.

Oak Bluffs. Above: A view of the harbor. Opposite: Porch rockers mark the unhurried pace of the Camp Ground and Fourth Avenue. Overleaf: Chinese and Japanese lanterns dominate the annual Illumination.

The Flea Market, Vineyard Have

A profusion of wildflowers proclaims the fullness of the Chilmark summer.

Menemsha. Above: The Pond, looking toward
the bight. Below: The jetty. Right: The harbor.

Below: Captain Rasmus Klimm's boathouse, Menemsha Harbor. Right: Reflections in Menemsha Pond.

Left: A grass-grown hull bears witness to past exchanges between land and sea.

Right: Baptist church, Gay Head.

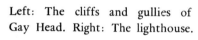
Left: The cliffs and gullies of Gay Head. Right: The lighthouse.

Time and weather have chiseled the many-colored clays of the Gay Head cliffs.

Herring Creek.

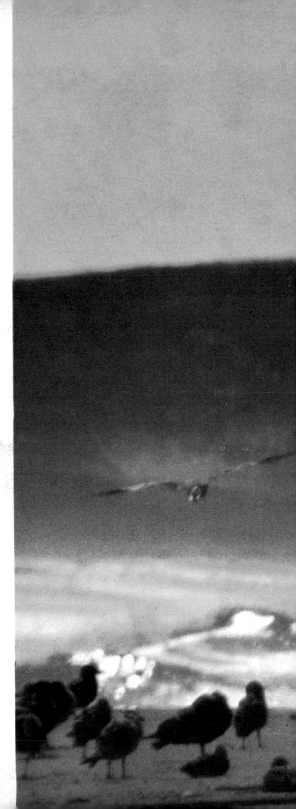

Above: Sand and sky meet along the dunes of Zack's Beach.
Right: Gulls come to rest on the beach near Squibnocket Point.

Exploring the quiet backwaters of Chilmark Pond.